A Beginning-to-Read Book

EARTH SCIENCE

DAYLIGHT AND DARKNESS

by Mary Lindeen

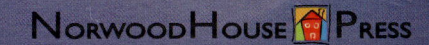

NORWOOD HOUSE PRESS

DEAR CAREGIVER,

The *Beginning to Read—Read and Discover Science* books provide young readers the opportunity to learn about scientific concepts while simultaneously building early reading skills. Each title corresponds to three of the key domains within the Next Generation Science Standards (NGSS): physical sciences, life sciences, and earth and space sciences.

The NGSS include standards that are comprised of three dimensions: Cross-cutting Concepts, Science and Engineering Practices, and Disciplinary Core Ideas. The texts within the *Read and Discover Science* series focus primarily upon the Disciplinary Core Ideas and Cross-cutting Concepts—helping readers view their world through a scientific lens. They pique a young reader's curiosity and encourage them to inquire and explore. The Connecting Concepts section at the back of each book offers resources to continue the exploration. The reinforcement activities at the back of the book support Science and Engineering Practices—to understand how scientists investigate phenomena in that world.

These easy-to-read informational texts make the scientific concepts accessible to young readers and prompt them to consider the role of science in their world. On one hand, these titles can develop background knowledge for exploring new topics. Alternately, they can be used to investigate, explain, and expand the findings of one's own inquiry. As you read with your child, encourage her or him to "observe"—taking notice of the images and information to formulate both questions and responses about what, how, and why something is happening.

Above all, the most important part of the reading experience is to have fun and enjoy it!

Sincerely,

Shannon Cannon

Shannon Cannon, Ph.D.
Literacy Consultant

Norwood House Press
For more information about Norwood House Press please visit our website at www.norwoodhousepress.com or call 866-565-2900.
© 2019 Norwood House Press. Beginning-to-Read™ is a trademark of Norwood House Press. All rights reserved. No part of this book may be reproduced or utilized in any form or by any means without written permission from the publisher.

Editor: Judy Kentor Schmauss
Designer: Lindaanne Donohoe

Photo Credits:

Shutterstock, 1, 3, 4-5, 6-7, 8-9, 10-11, 12-13, 14-15, 18, 19, 20-21, 22-23, 24-25, 26-27; iStock Photo, 16, 17

Library of Congress Cataloging-in-Publication Data

Names: Lindeen, Mary, author.
Title: Daylight and darkness / by Mary Lindeen.
Description: Chicago, IL : Norwood House Press, [2018] | Series: A beginning to read book | Audience: K to grade 3.
Identifiers: LCCN 2018009105 (print) | LCCN 2018004469 (ebook) | ISBN 9781684041534 (eBook) | ISBN 9781599538976 (library edition : alk. paper)
Subjects: LCSH: Day–Juvenile literature. | Night–Juvenile literature. | Light and darkness–Juvenile literature. | Seasons–Juvenile literature. | Earth (Planet)–Rotation–Juvenile literature.
Classification: LCC QB633 (print) | LCC QB633 .L5275 2018 (ebook) | DDC 535–dc23
LC record available at https://lccn.loc.gov/2018009105

Hardcover ISBN: 978-1-59953-897-6   Paperback ISBN: 978-1-68404-144-2

344R-082021
Manufactured in the United States of America in North Mankato, Minnesota.

Good morning!
Here comes the sun.
It's time to wake up.

4

The sun rises every morning.

We call this time of day sunrise.

The sun is high in the sky at noon.

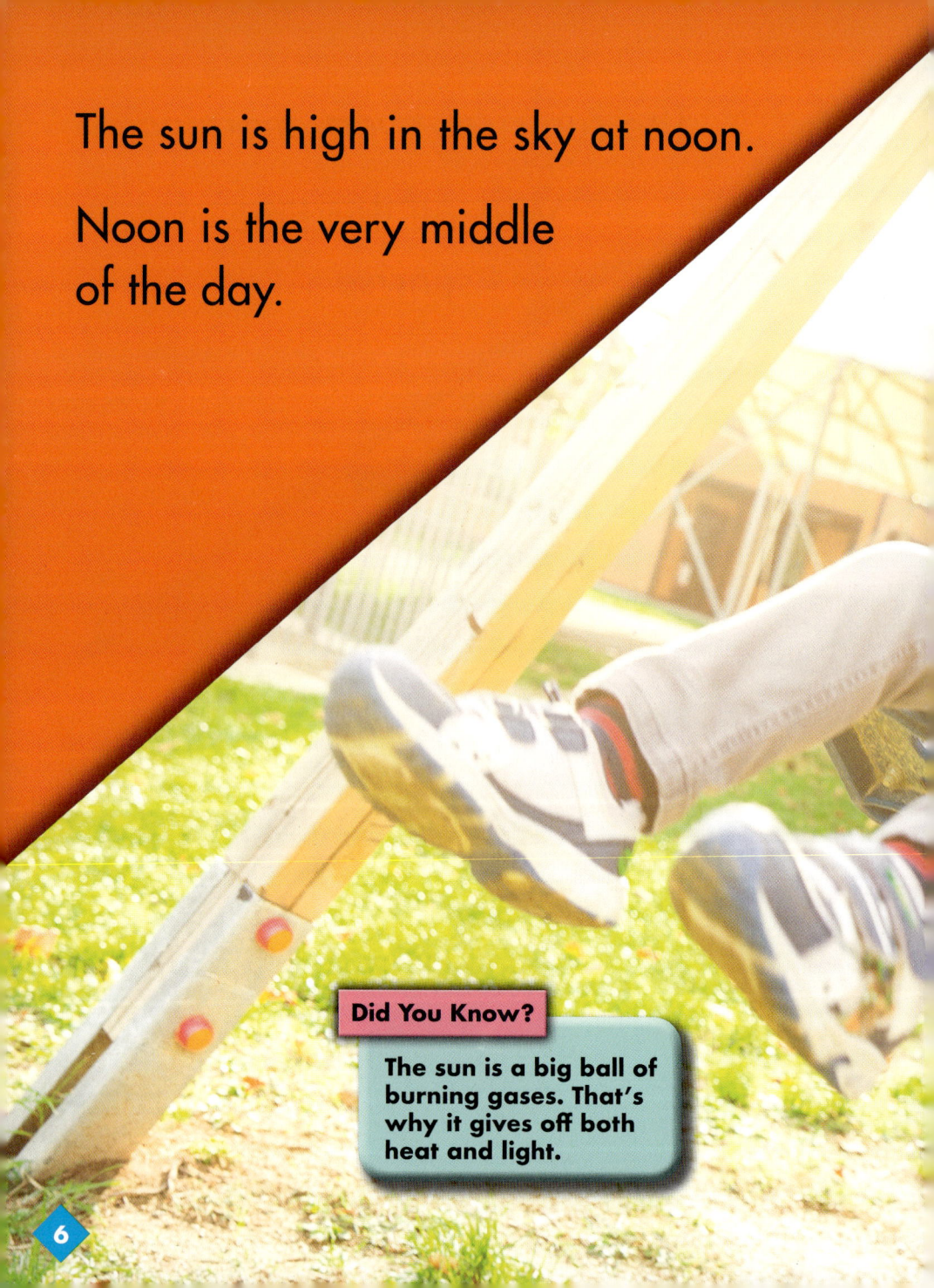

Noon is the very middle of the day.

Did You Know?

The sun is a big ball of burning gases. That's why it gives off both heat and light.

7

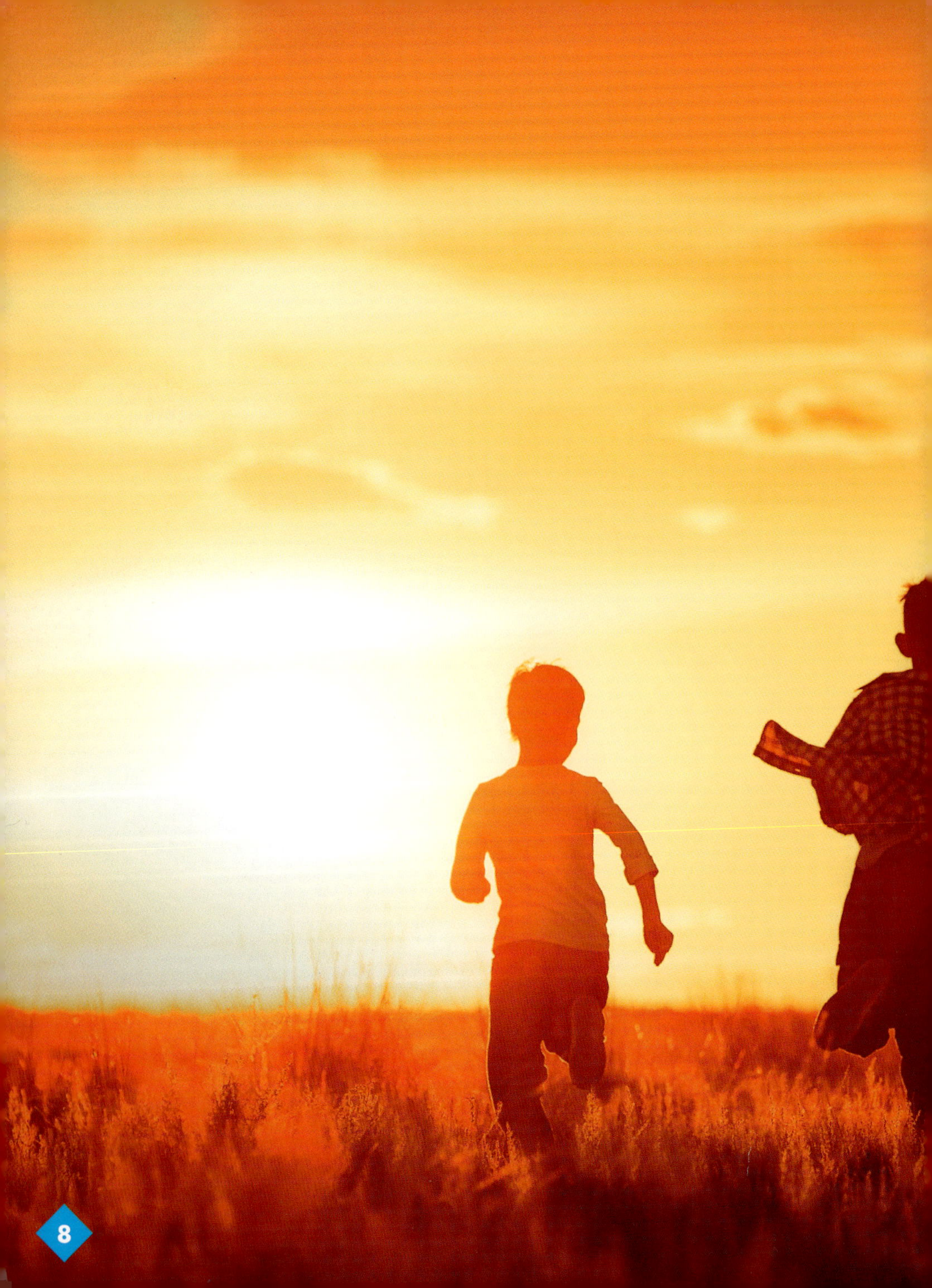

The sun starts to go down every evening.

This time of day is called sunset.

Then the sun disappears from view.

The sky is dark.

It's night.

Did You Know?

The moon does not make its own light. It reflects light from the sun.

11

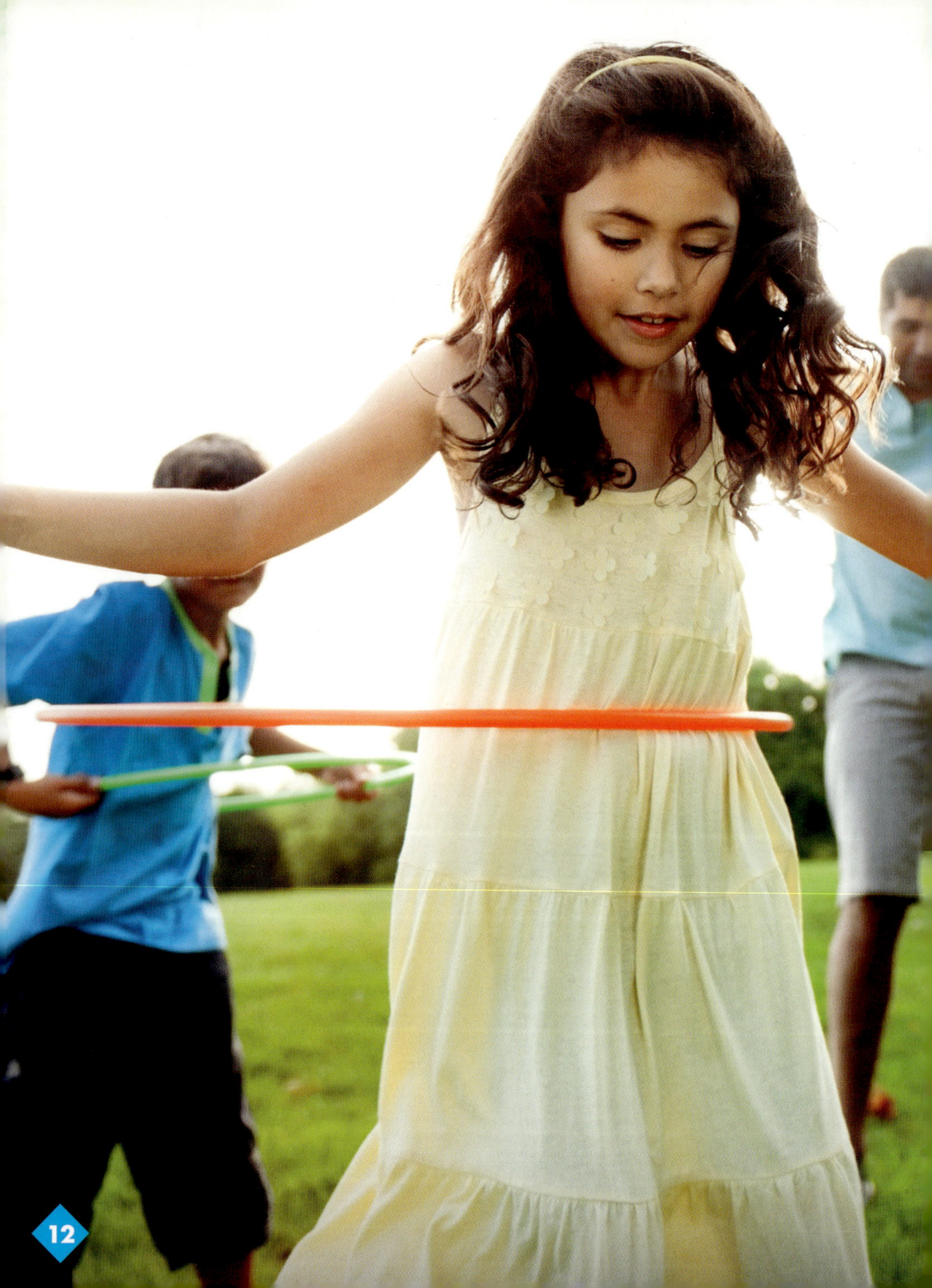

We have some daylight every day.

The amount of daylight we have each day changes.

It changes with the seasons.

15

Winter days have less daylight than other days in the year.

The sun rises later.

It might still be dark outside when you wake up in the morning.

The sun sets earlier, too.

Spring days have more daylight than winter days do.

The sun rises a little earlier.

It sets a little later.

20

Summer days have the most daylight.

The sunrise is much earlier each day.

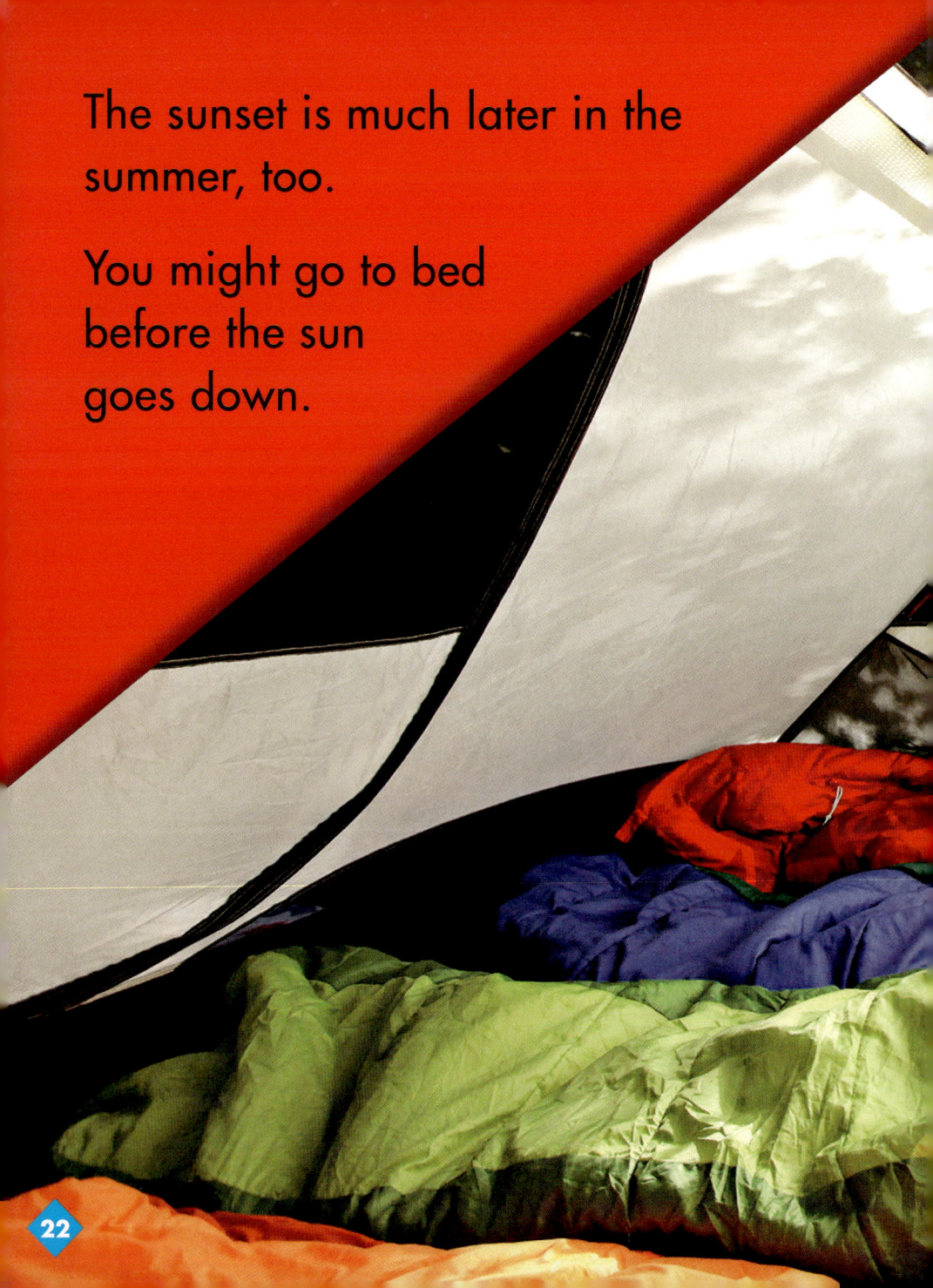

The sunset is much later in the summer, too.

You might go to bed before the sun goes down.

23

Fall days have less daylight than summer days.

The sun rises later.

It sets earlier.

25

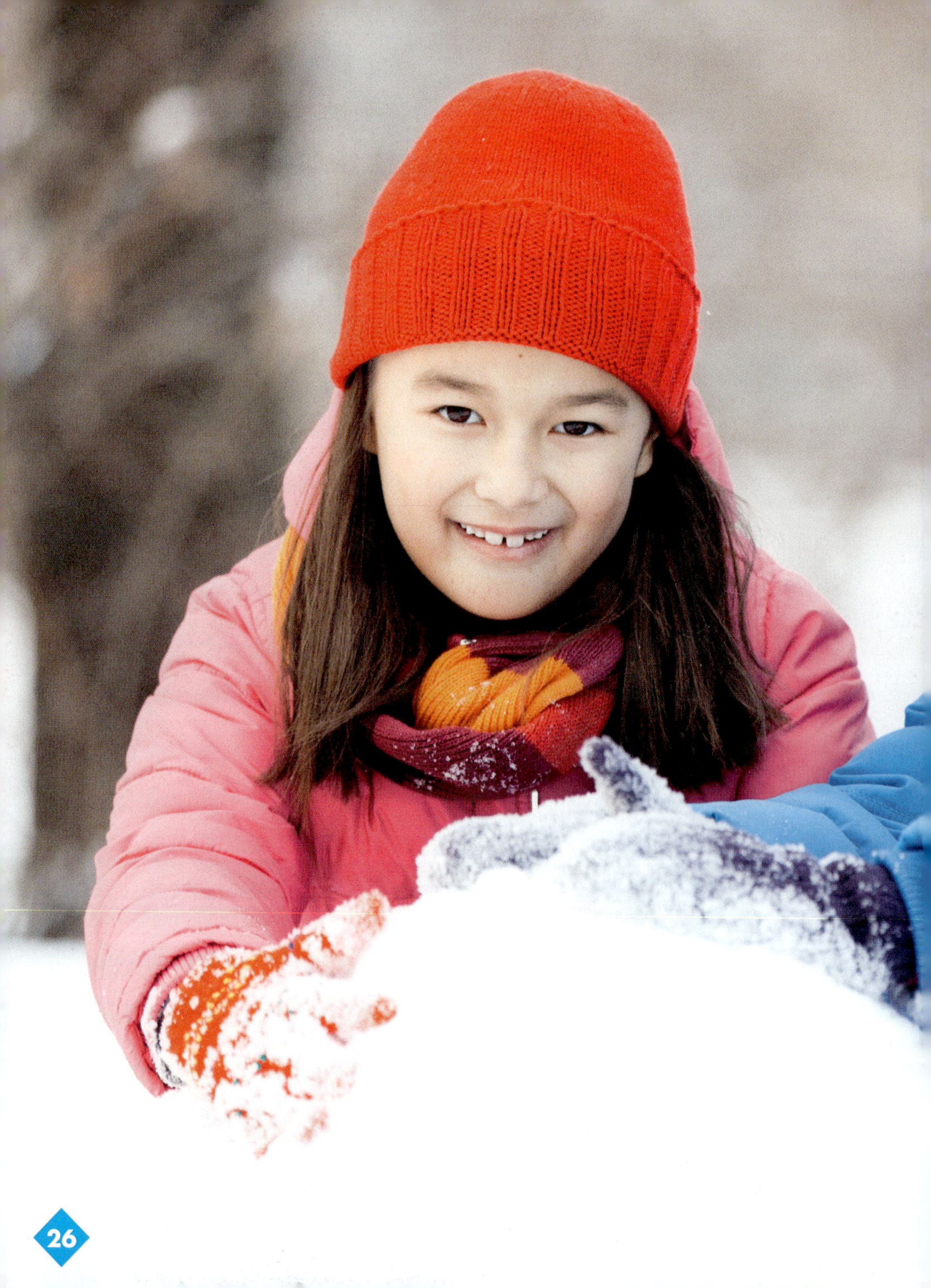

After fall, winter comes again.

The seasons go on and on.

Daylight and darkness change all year long.

What can you observe about daylight and darkness where you live?

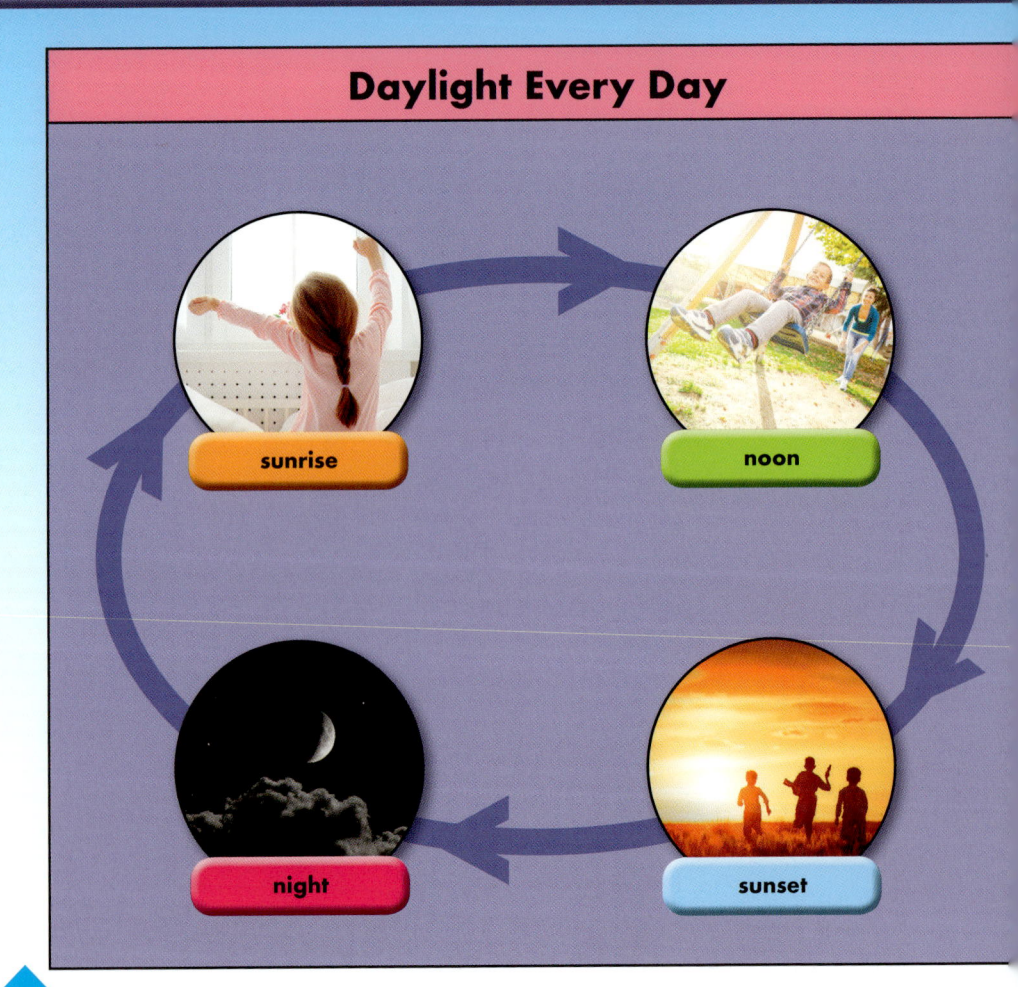

Daylight Every Day

sunrise

noon

sunset

night

Daylight Every Season

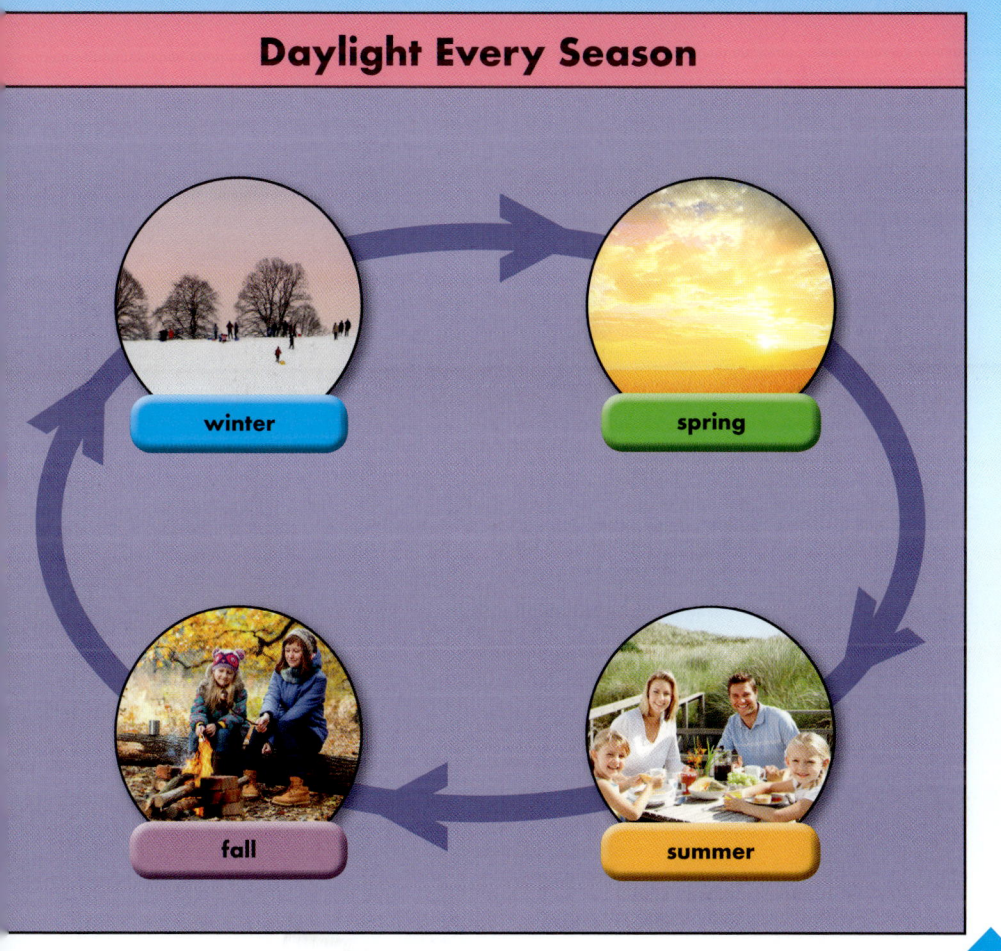

winter

spring

fall

summer

EARTH SCIENCE

CONNECTING CONCEPTS

CLOSE READING OF NONFICTION TEXT

Close reading helps children comprehend text. It includes reading a text, discussing it with others, and answering questions about it. Use these questions to discuss this book with your child:

- What is sunrise? When does it happen?
- How would you explain the change in the amount of daylight we get throughout the year?
- Why does the sun seem to disappear at night?
- How would you explain what noon is?
- What did the author want you to learn from this book?

SCIENCE IN THE REAL WORLD

Keep track of the times the sun rises and sets for a week. At the end of the week, share what you learned.

SCIENCE AND ACADEMIC LANGUAGE

Make sure your child understands the meaning of the following words:

disappears   gases   reflects   rises

Have him or her use the words in a sentence.

FLUENCY

Help your child practice fluency by using one or more of the following activities:

- Reread the book to your child at least two times while he or she uses a finger to track each word as it is read.
- Read a line of the book, then reread it as your child reads along with you.
- Ask your child to go back through the book and read the words he or she knows.
- Have your child practice reading the book several times to improve accuracy, rate, and expression.

FOR FURTHER INFORMATION

Books:

Demuth, Patricia Brennan. *The Sun: Our Amazing Star*. New York, NY: Grosset & Dunlap, 2016.

Evans, Shira. *Day and Night*. Washington, DC: National Geographic Kids, 2016.

Nelson, Robin. *Day and Night*. Minneapolis, MN: Lerner, 2010.

Websites:

Annenberg Learner: Why Does the Sun Rise and Set?
DK Find Out: Day and Night
https://www.dkfindout.com/us/space/solar-system/day-and-night/

PBS Learning Media: Observe Sunrise and Sunset
https://www.pbslearningmedia.org/resource/ess05.sci.ess.eiu.riseset/observe-sunrise-and-sunset/#.WiV_-baZMW8

Word List

Daylight and Darkness uses the 103 words listed below. *High-frequency words* are those words that are used most often in the English language. They are sometimes referred to as sight words because children need to learn to recognize them automatically when they read. *Content words* are any words specific to a particular topic. Regular practice reading these words will enhance your child's ability to read with greater fluency and comprehension.

High-Frequency Words

a	both	from	its	off	this	why
about	call(ed)	give(s)	little	on	time	with
after	can	go(es)	long	other	to	year
again	come(s)	good	make	own	too	you
all	day(s)	have	might	set(s)	up	
and	do	here	more	some	very	
at	does	high	most	still	we	
be	down	in	much	than	what	
before	each	is	not	the	when	
big	every	it	of	then	where	

Content Words

amount	daylight	heat	middle	outside	starts	view
ball	disappears	it's	moon	reflects	summer	wake
bed	earlier	later	morning	rises	sun	winter
burning	evening	less	night	seasons	sunrise	
change(s)	fall	light	noon	sky	sunset	
dark(ness)	gases	live	observe	spring	that's	

About the Author

Mary Lindeen is a writer, editor, parent, and former elementary school teacher. She has written more than 100 books for children and edited many more. She specializes in early literacy instruction and books for young readers, especially nonfiction.

About the Advisor

Dr. Shannon Cannon is an elementary school teacher in Sacramento, California. She has served as a teacher educator in the School of Education at UC Davis, where she also earned her Ph.D. in Language, Literacy, and Culture. As a member of the clinical faculty, she supervised pre-service teachers and taught elementary methods courses in reading, effective teaching, and teacher action research.